For John

Ellen B. Senisi's many
photo-essay books include
the award-winning JUST KIDS.
Ms. Senisi lives in Schenectady,
New York, with her husband,
John, and her children,
Kate, Will, and Steven.

Special thanks to Mrs. Felthousen
and all her children at Yates
Arts-in-Education Magnet School
in Schenectady, New York.

Hurray for Pre-K!
Copyright © 2000 by Ellen B. Senisi
Printed in the U.S.A.
All rights reserved.
www.harperchildrens.com

Library of Congress
  Cataloging-in-Publication Data
Senisi, Ellen B.
  Hurray for pre-K! / text and photographs
by Ellen B. Senisi.
      p.   cm.
  Summary: A child describes a day in
pre-K, playing, snacking, resting, singing,
and painting.
  ISBN 0-06-028896-5
  ISBN 0-06-028897-3 (lib. bdg.)
  [1.Nursery schools—Fiction.   2. Schools—
Fiction.]   I. Title.
PZ7.S4726Hu   2000   99-45405
[E]—dc21   CIP
                                   AC

Typography by Matt Adamec
1 2 3 4 5 6 7 8 9 10
❖ First Edition

Hurray for Pre-K!

**Text and Photographs by
Ellen B. Senisi**

HarperCollinsPublishers

come

I come in.
I see my friends.

come come come

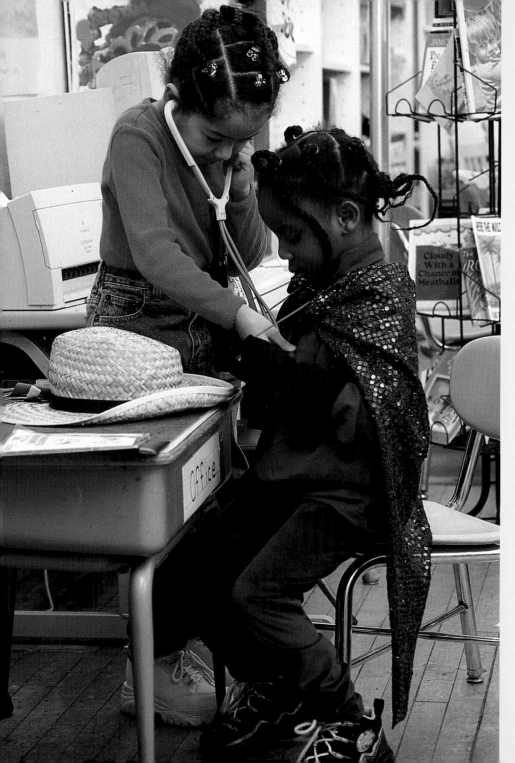

play

I play a lot.
Sometimes I play
by myself and
sometimes I play
with my friends.

play play play

pretend

I can pretend to be someone else.

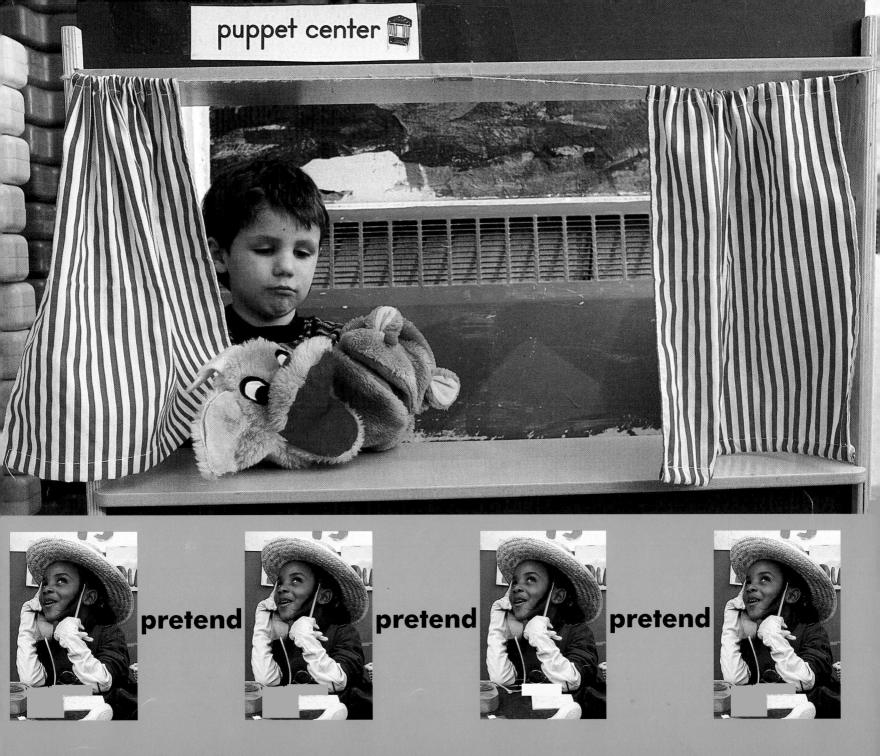

puppet center

pretend pretend pretend

clean

When playtime is done, we all clean up.

clean

clean

clean

eat

We eat snack.

eat eat eat

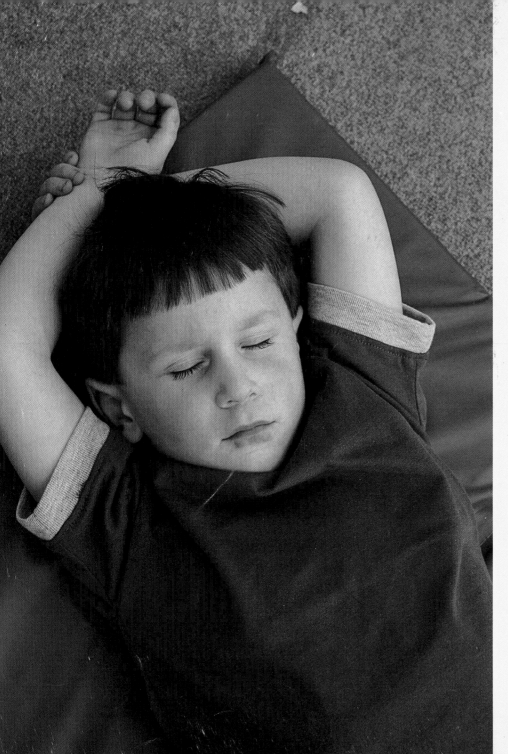

rest

Sometimes I rest.
Sometimes I don't.

rest   rest   rest

feel

I feel happy at school. If I feel sad, I can ask someone to help me.

feel feel feel

read

I love to **read**.

read   read   read

listen

We listen when our teacher talks.

listen   listen   listen

sing

We **sing** together.
We play instruments
and move to music.

sing **sing** **sing**

help

I help my friends
and they help me.

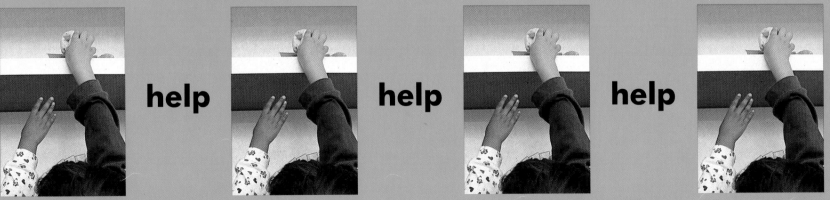

help   help   help

make

I make things in school all by myself.

make make make

paint

I paint in beautiful colors. I can take my artwork home when I leave.

paint   paint   paint

go

I go home.

go

go

go

be

I can **be** myself
in Pre-K.

be **be** **be**

Hurray for Pre-K!

come

play

pretend

clean

eat

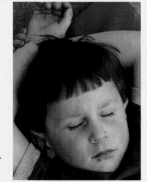
rest

feel

read

listen

sing

help

make

paint

go

be